FUSING GLASS MADE SIMPLE

A COMPLETE GUIDE ON SIMPLE GLASS FUSING

GLENN CARTER

Table of Contents

CHAPTER ONE

Fusing Glass: A Complete Guide

Fusing glass opens up a world of design possibilities, allowing you to create both useful objects and beautiful works of art. It's important to learn how glass reacts to heat, and how to cut and fuse glass safely.

What is the process of glass fusing?

To fuse glass, compatible sheets of glass are placed in a kiln at a temperature of approximately 1490 degrees Fahrenheit and heated until the glass fuses together. It gives you the ability to create stunning, one-of-a-kind works of glass art. Due to the fact that the glass is cold, you can spend as much time as necessary working on your designs because you are working with it at all times.

What is fused glass, and how does it differ from regular glass?

When two or more pieces of glass are heated in a kiln, the result is a single piece of fused glass.

Glass fusing is an art form.

You can use fused glass to make everything from plates and tiles to jewelry and wall art. Creating a finished piece of fused glass requires only a kiln and some simple tools. Bulk production of vessels and other objects that are difficult or impossible to fabricate in a kiln uses glass blowing. Using a large furnace to melt the glass and a variety of other tools is necessary to complete the glass blowing process. A mold is used to make a three-dimensional sculpture out of cast glass, which is then fired in a kiln and coldworked with grinders and polishers. A torch is used in glass flameworking to create a finished object, but the process can only handle smaller items.

Before You Begin

Glass that is easily combustible

When it comes to fusing, the type of glass you use is critical.

It must be a type of glass that can withstand the heat and cold cycles of the kiln.

Sorry to say, but this means that you won't be able to use any of your scraps from other projects to make fused art.

For successful fusion, each piece must be compatible with the others.

Known as 'Fusible Glass', Bullseye and Spectrum produce the most popular lines. System 96 is the name given to Spectrum's fusing range.

When heated, glass behaves in a similar way.

1/4inch is the ideal thickness for fused glass (6mm).

You can no longer get an exact square piece of 1/8 (3mm) sheetglass after firing it in a kiln.

Three layers (3/8inch/9mm) of glass would melt and push outward, resulting in a rounded and larger square.

Is there a second layer? Perfect. The glass is square and has a constant size.

What You'll Need to Get Started

Fusible glass, patterns, glass cutters, grozing pliers, detergent cleaners, safety glasses, dustpans and brushes, and a kiln are all required.

A grinder can be added as an option.

How to make a glass fusing torch

Fused glass can take you anywhere you want to go once you have the right tools and safety precautions in place in your studio. If you prefer, you can fuse it flat or add a variety of textures, including mixed media. Making slumped glass art begins with fusing the material. To get started with glass fusing, follow the simple instructions listed below.

To begin, you'll need to organize your workspace.

Gather the necessary materials and equipment for cutting glass. Use a kiln wash or firing paper to line the shelf of your kiln.

Second, get your drink ready.

Shape the glass to your liking. However, if you'd prefer a smoother finish, you can always grind down the edges of your pieces. Check to see that the glass is free of smudges and fingerprints before using it. In the kiln, dirty glass can cause the piece to be marked by smudges, which can be difficult to remove.

- Step 3: Put together your glass

Take care to ensure that your work is not too close to the kiln shelf or other projects when putting it in. For more complex designs, we recommend using a small amount of glue to affix the pieces together. Even a light sprinkling can help ensure that your design remains intact when your piece(s) are loaded into the kiln.

CHAPTER TWO

- Step 4: Burn your piece of art.
-

The kiln should be fired to the correct temperature and schedule. The glass should be completely cool before you remove your piece.

- Step 5: Take a look at your work of art!

Observe your stunning work of fusing glass! Slumping your fused glass requires inspecting the edges for any rough or sharp spots. If you discover any sharp edges that require grinding, begin at the backside and work your way forward with a grinder or diamond hand pad.

• Step 6: Glass slumping is optional.

The piece must be carefully placed on the mold and heated to the slumping temperature before being slumped. Aside from that, the piece is complete and ready to be displayed or put to good use. Make sure to wash any fused glass by hand and handle it with caution.

This pattern was created by Daniel using a patterned bar flow fusing. Fused glass is made by heating strips of glass that are stacked and then placing them in a dam in the kiln.

She fused and slumped the glass to create patterns and depth. Copper accents were also used by the artist.

Fusing glass: a beginner's guide

Many online resources exist, but the best way to learn is to attend a class. With the guidance of an experienced glass artist, taking a fusing class will ensure your safety and allow you to produce the best work possible. If you're just getting started, an in-person class will be less expensive than buying and setting up your own home glass fusing studio. Taking an in-person class before deciding to open your own studio is a good idea because of the high costs involved.

At The Crucible, you can learn how to fuse glass.

Classes at The Crucible teach you how to heat and reshape glass in a kiln to create art or useful items like plates and bowls. Painting on glass and using recycled materials are just a few of the techniques you'll learn in our one-on-one classes. The Crucible is the perfect place to experiment with glass-draping and glass-fusing techniques. Whether you're looking for a quick introduction to the art of glass fusing or a more in-depth course like Glass Fusing or Slumping, we have a class for you. Kiln Formed Glass or a self-guided Glass Fusing and Slumping Lab can be added to your repertoire once you have the basics down.

FAQs on glass fusion

What type of glass should I use for fusing glass?

Fusing soda-lime glass is common because of the wide temperature range of the kiln and the wide variety of accessory glass that can be used in design. Frit, stringers, and dichroic glass are a few of the options (metal fused to the glass in a vacuum chamber). The COE (coefficient of expansion) of float (window glass) glass is different than that of soda-lime glass, so the fusing temperatures and times will differ.

The melting point of soda-lime glass is between 1350 and 1500 degrees Fahrenheit. Soda-lime glass fuses at a lower temperature than float glass.

A computerized controller or pyrometer that displays the kiln's temperature is necessary, as is a suitable kiln. Having cutting tools and a glass grinder in your home studio is also a good idea.

If I want to fuse glass, I'm wondering how long it will take.

Smaller pieces can be completed in three to four hours, while larger ones can take up to 13-14 hours, depending on the thickness and size of the glass used. Glass must be cooled to 900–1000 degrees Fahrenheit after fusing to relieve any stress that may have been built up during the firing procedure.

Beginner's Guide to Glass Fusing

Using fusing glass, you can create a wide range of objects for a wide range of uses. In this article, we'll give you a variety of glass fusing ideas so that you can experiment with new materials and techniques when working with glass again.

It doesn't take a lot of materials or equipment to make a fusing glass piece. Fusible glass, a kiln, and appropriate safety gear are all you need to get started.

Glass fusing is a great hobby for those who have never done it before, but if you're just getting started, we recommend reading this article on the basics of fusing glass to learn more about the materials you can use, how to do it correctly, and what kind of kiln you should get based on the pieces you'll be making.

A few suggestions for glass fusing:

Plates

Tableware, such as plates and spoons, must be made from FDA-approved fusible glass if you want to use it to cook or eat with. Usually this information is displayed on the label, package or website of the glass.

Plates in strips

Square or rectangular fusible glass strips placed next to each other and then melted in a kiln form strip plates. You must ensure that the pieces of glass you are working with melt at the same temperature in order to get the best results from this process. If this is not the case, the plate may break once it has cooled.

With the help of kiln shelves, you can create a perfect square or rectangle. Flat plates and coasters can be made for display purposes. Molds, on the other hand, can be used to give them a slight curve, making them more functional.

As an example, consider these strip plate glass fusing designs:

Construction of a sheet of glass fusing strips

Striped bowl in green and red

plate with a kaleidoscope of hues

Plates of the standard variety

Avoid strips if you're looking for something simpler and less time-consuming. Simple plates can be made from melted glass panels of various colors. Consider the following:

CHAPTER THREE

Red dichroic glass highlights a purple plate.

Plate depicting the beach and ocean in a piece of fused glass

Plate of fused glass made of lime and cobalt

Three types of jewelry are included: necklaces and earrings, as well as rings

Fusing glass allows you to make a wide variety of jewelry. Using a variety of fusing techniques, colors, and textures, you can create your own unique glass pendants. Use gold or silver chains and hooks to make fancy necklaces, earrings and rings or just use leather for a more rustic appearance.

Here are a few concepts to get you started:

Fused glass necklace in the color of green dichroic

Necklace pendant made of fused glass

Intricately carved wood jewelry case

Earrings in the picasso style of dichroic glass

Whiskey Sniffer

This is a simple glass fusing idea for beginners, if not the simplest. Drinks are stirred with swizzle sticks. Using the same fusible glass strips that we discussed earlier, you can create these beautiful pieces of art.

Melting a few strips of different colors will do the trick if this is your first time working with a torch. You can also create multicolor swizzle sticks by building a stick out of several small pieces of glass of different colors. Consider the following:

Red abstract swizzle sticks made of fused glass

Gold metallic flakes adorn these cocktail stirrers made of glass.

Swirly cocktail sticks in a rainbow of hues

Stakes for the Garden

To support newly planted trees, label different plants and flowers, divide your garden into different zones, or simply decorate your front or back yard, you can use wooden or metal posts to create functional and beautiful-looking garden stakes. Here are a few concepts for designs:

Garden stake with a fusing glass butterfly design

a collection of variously patterned garden stakes

Imaginative garden stakes in cartoon form

Stakes for birds in the garden

Ideas for Christmas Ornaments Made with Fused Glass

Making your own Christmas tree ornaments sounds awesome, doesn't it? Well, this year is your year to make it happen!

To hang your finished ornaments, you'll need either hooks or metallic cords used for decorating and gift wrapping, in addition to a variety of fusible glass in various colors. These include candles, bells, birds and wreaths, as well as mini trees, santa, angels, gifts, and candy canes, which are the most common designs. Consider the following:

Christmas gnome in red, white, and green

Glass soldiers made of fused glass.

Christmas decorations with glass-fused birds

Additional Ornaments

As in the making of Christmas tree ornaments, you can transform your pieces with the help of additional materials into whatever you desire.

Small magnets can be purchased and used for making fridge magnets, key chains, or even wall art. Here are a few more suggestions for glass fusing:

Fused glass artwork depicting a cosmological fish

Fused glass wall sconces depicting trees

Rainbow fusing glass keyring

To create fused glass art, you'll need these tools.

Our glass fusing 101 guide has all the information you need about the supplies, tools, and materials you need to fuse glass if you need help or advice on what to get for your next projects.

A glass kiln is required if you want to properly fuse glass. A kiln is a type of oven that is specifically designed to dry and melt clay and glass. Depending on the number of pieces you intend to make, you can choose from a variety of sizes.

As an example, microwave kilns typically have a chamber with a diameter of up to 6 inches and work very effectively. On average, they're able to melt small pieces of glass in under ten minutes. If you're only going to be fusing a few small pieces of glass at a time, this is the most cost-effective method for you.

A large electric glass kiln is by far the best option for anyone who intends to regularly fuse glass, whether as a hobby or as a profession.

Hope you enjoyed our glass fusing inspirations! Best of luck!

THE END